Writing Builders

Jesse and Jasmine Build a
JOURNAL

by Rachel Lynette
illustrated by Carlos Aón

Content Consultant
Jan Lacina, Ph.D.
College of Education
Texas Christian University

NORWOOD HOUSE PRESS
CHICAGO, ILLINOIS

P.O. Box 316598
Chicago, Illinois 60631
For information regarding Norwood House Press, please visit
our website at:
www.norwoodhousepress.com or call 866-565-2900.

Editor: Melissa York
Designer: Craig Hinton
Project Management: Red Line Editorial

Library of Congress Cataloging-in-Publication Data
Lynette, Rachel.
  Jesse and Jasmine build a journal / by Rachel Lynette ;
illustrated by Carlos Aon.
     pages cm.
  Includes bibliographical references.
  Summary: "Jesse and Jasmine learn to write a journal while
taking a trip to Yellowstone National Park. The journals include
pictures, lists, and narratives on the fun and danger they faced.
Activities in the back help the reader start their own journal"--
Provided by publisher.
  ISBN 978-1-59953-585-2 (library edition : alk. paper)
  ISBN 978-1-60357-565-2 (ebook)
  1. Diaries--Authorship--Juvenile literature. I. Aon, Carlos. II.
Title.
  PN4390.L95 2013
  372.62'3--dc23
                                2013010271

Words in **black bold** are defined in the glossary.

Journaling Journey

Last summer, my family went on a camping trip to Yellowstone National Park. At the start of the trip, my mom gave my brother and me each a journal. At first, I wasn't too excited about the idea. The book had a lot of pages, and I couldn't imagine filling them all with writing. Luckily, it wasn't as hard as I thought. It was fun!

I liked journaling so much I decided to keep writing even after we got home from our trip. Last night, I wrote about being in our school's holiday concert. Here is the cool part—that **entry** was on the last page of the book. I really did fill up all those pages! Today, Mom is taking me to the store to buy a new journal. Then we are going out for ice cream!

By Jasmine, age 9

"And away we go!" Mr. Davis said as he backed the minivan out of the driveway.

"Yippee!" called Jesse and Jasmine from the backseat. After all the planning and packing, the Davis family was finally on the way to Yellowstone National Park. "How long until we get there, Dad?" Jesse asked.

"It's a long drive," Mr. Davis replied. "But if we drive all day, we should make it by dinnertime."

Jasmine groaned, but Jesse said, "Don't worry—we've got games, movies, and puzzle books. We'll be fine."

"And I have something else to help you pass the time," said Mrs. Davis from the front seat. She handed each of her children a pencil and a book: a blue one for Jesse and a purple one for Jasmine.

Jasmine opened hers to find that the pages were all blank. "How am I supposed to read a book with no writing?" she asked.

"It's a journal," Mrs. Davis replied. "I thought it would be fun for you to write about the trip. That way you can read it later and remember what we did."

"Neat!" Jesse said. "We kept **personal journals** in school last year. I bet you will next year too, Jasmine."

Jasmine flipped through the blank pages. "There sure are a lot of pages," she said.

"I think you'll be surprised at how the book fills up," Mrs. Davis said. "And you can draw pictures too."

"Well, I am a good artist," Jasmine said. "And I like writing too. This will be fun!"

Jasmine opened her journal to the first page and wrote:

We are on our way to Yellowstone National Park. We are going to camp there for a whole week. Mom gave me this journal so that I can write about everything we see.

"Umm, I have a problem," Jasmine said.

"You don't have to go to the bathroom already, do you?" asked Mr. Davis.

"No, it's just that we haven't done anything but ride in the van, so I don't have anything to write about yet."

"Why don't you make a list?" Jesse suggested. "You could make a list of everything you want to do on the trip."

"Am I allowed?" Jasmine asked. "I thought that a journal was for writing down things that have already happened."

"It's fine," Jesse assured her. "My teacher had us do lists all the time. She said that lists help you organize your ideas. And also, you may end up writing about some of the things you put on your list later, after we do them."

"Well, there are all kinds of things I want to do on our trip, so this should be easy." Jasmine began to write again. When she was done, she read her list out loud.

Things I want to do at Yellowstone

1. See a bison
2. See a moose
3. NOT see a bear!
4. See Old Faithful erupt
5. Go on a hike
6. Learn to make a campfire
7. Toast marshmallows and make s'mores— Yum!

"Great start!" Mrs. Davis said. "Here, take a look at this and see if you want to add a few more things to your list." She passed a book back to Jasmine. It was called *Yellowstone National Park: A Guidebook.*

Jasmine looked through the book. There were lots of interesting pictures. She added to her list:

8. See the geysers and the hot springs with the pretty rainbow colors
9. See the mud volcanoes
10. Become a junior ranger

"Looks like you have a great list there," her brother said when she showed it to him. "Now just date your entry and you will be done."

"Good idea. That way if I read this again when I am older, I will know when we took this trip." Jasmine wrote the date carefully in the upper right-hand corner. Then she closed her journal and put it away in her travel backpack.

Jasmine and Jesse spent the rest of the drive playing games and watching movies. By the time they got to their campground, everyone was ready to get out of the car! Jasmine helped Mr. Davis set up the tent while Jesse and Mrs. Davis made dinner.

Jasmine forgot about her journal until she found it at the bottom of her backpack just before bed. She wanted to write about the day, but Mrs. Davis said no. They had a big day planned and Jasmine would need a good night's sleep.

Mrs. Davis was right, and the next day was jam-packed. That night, Jasmine wrote about it in her journal. Then she drew a picture of Old Faithful erupting. The next day, the family went to see a giant waterfall. Mr. Davis took lots of pictures.

"I wish we didn't have to wait until we get home to print the pictures," Jesse said while they were eating lunch. "I'd like to put one of this waterfall in my journal and write about it."

"I bet we could buy a postcard with a picture of the waterfall in one of the gift shops," said Mr. Davis. "Would that do the trick?"

"Sure," said Jesse. "Maybe Jasmine will want one too."

They stopped at a gift shop and Jesse and Jasmine each picked out a postcard. Jesse picked one of the waterfall, and Jasmine chose one of a bison. When they got back to camp, they glued their postcards into their journals.

August 7, 2014

Today we saw a lot of geysers. Geysers are kind of like small volcanoes, except instead of erupting with lava, they shoot hot water and steam into the air. One of the biggest geysers was Old Faithful. We had to wait about 20 minutes for it to erupt, but it was really cool when it did. Then we had lunch at the Old Faithful Lodge. I had grilled cheese. I love grilled cheese. Jesse had a hamburger. We saw lots of other geysers and hot springs. Dad took tons of pictures. Then we came back to our campsite and had spaghetti for dinner and s'mores for dessert! It was a good day.

Jasmine wrote:

August 8, 2014
This is a bison. We saw some bison crossing the road today.

Then she didn't know what else to write. She saw Jesse was still writing. "How can you write so much about a picture?"

"Well," he said, "I'm not just writing about the picture. I'm also writing about my thoughts and how the picture **relates** to me. That way I will be able to remember why I wrote about it in the first place."

He handed his journal to Jasmine. Jasmine read:

August 8, 2014
Today we went to see this waterfall. It is the lower part of Yellowstone Falls. This is what it looks like from the top, but we went down a bunch of stairs to get even closer to the falls. It was really amazing. It was all misty at the bottom. It was the biggest and loudest waterfall I have ever seen (and heard).

"Oh, I get it now. It's neat how you wrote about how loud it was because you can't tell that from the picture." Jasmine picked up her pencil again and added:

You can't tell from the picture, but bison are really big! I know because today I saw one up close. We were driving back to camp when all the cars on the road stopped. Some bison were in the middle of the road! It was a little scary, but Dad said if we didn't bother them and stayed in the car, they wouldn't bother us. That turned out to be true since I am here writing this journal entry and not flat from being stepped on by a giant bison.

The next day, the family moved to a different campground in another part of the park. Jesse and Jasmine went off to explore, but soon Jasmine came back alone. She shuffled into the campsite with a big frown on her face. "What's wrong, Jasmine?" Mrs. Davis asked.

"We met some kids from another campsite," Jasmine replied glumly. "They were all Jesse's age, and some were even older. They said Jesse could hang out with them, but not me because I am too little."

"I'm sorry," Mrs. Davis replied. "It can be really hard to be the little sister sometimes. You know what might help?"

"What?" asked Jasmine.

"Your journal. Sometimes writing about a problem or something that has upset you can make you feel better. Then if you want, we can talk about it over a cup of hot chocolate."

Jasmine got out her journal. She wrote in fast, angry sentences:

August 9, 2014

It's not fair! Those kids wouldn't let me play with them and Jesse didn't do anything. He should have stayed with me instead of going off with them. He is the worst brother ever!!!!

Well, not really. Usually he is really nice to me. He helps me with my homework and a lot of the time he lets me pick the TV channel. I guess he just really wanted to hang out with those kids. Maybe I could find some kids who are my age to play with.

By the time she was done writing, Jasmine did feel a lot better. Mrs. Davis handed Jasmine a steaming cup of hot chocolate. "Do you want to show me what you wrote?" she asked.

Jasmine shut her journal quickly. "I don't think so," she said. "It's kind of **private**."

"I understand," Mrs. Davis said. "That is one of the good things about a personal journal. You don't have to show it to anyone. I never let anyone see my journals when I was your age."

"You had a journal when you were younger?" Jasmine asked.

"I got my first journal for my tenth birthday and I wrote in it almost every day. I still have it too. I'll show it to you someday."

"That's really cool. I bet it is fun to read about yourself when you were my age."

"It is," Mrs. Davis replied. "And now you will get to do the same thing when you are my age!"

By the time Jesse came back, Jasmine was feeling much better. That night, he taught her how to build a campfire.

The next day, the family went on a hike in the backcountry. It took most of the day and they were tired when they got back to the car. They stopped at one of the park's restaurants for dinner. As they were getting out of the car, Jesse said, "Bring your journal in, Jasmine. I have an idea for us to try."

After they were seated and had ordered their food, Jesse explained his idea. "I thought it would be fun to try a Five-Minute Freewrite. That is when you write as fast as you can for five minutes. You can write about anything—just whatever pops into your head. And you don't have to worry about spelling or writing neatly. Want to try it?"

"Sure," Jasmine said as she opened her journal.

Mrs. Davis set the stopwatch on her cell phone for five minutes. "Ready . . . Set . . . Go!" she said, and both kids began to write fast. Jasmine wrote:

August 10, 2014
Today we went for a hike for five miles. Dad said we had to make lots of noise so that we would not surprise any bears, so we were always talking. Luckily, we did not see any bears, but we did see squirrels. I leave peanuts for the squirrels at home, but you can't feed the animals here. It's against the rules. I'm glad we wen

"Time's up!" Mrs. Davis said.

"Whew!" Jasmine said. "Can I go back and finish my last sentence?"

"Sure, it's your journal," replied Jesse.

Jasmine finished her sentence as dinner came.

I'm glad we went hiking, but I hope we do something with less walking tomorrow.

Jasmine continued to write in her journal for the rest of the trip. She wrote about the gloopy mud volcanoes, seeing mountain goats, and becoming a junior ranger. Sometimes she shared what she wrote with her family and other times she kept it to herself. On the last day of their trip, she wrote:

August 13, 2014

Today, we packed up our tent. I felt kind of sad because this has been a really fun trip and now it is almost over. But we did get to do nearly everything on my list and Dad says we can come back, maybe even next summer.

One cool thing that happened today is that we saw a moose. Jesse had really wanted to see a moose in the wild and we hadn't seen one yet. He was so excited! What was really neat was that we saw it near the edge of the park, right before we left. It was like it was there to say good-bye to us.

In a few hours, we will be home. I'm glad Mom gave me this journal. I don't want to ever forget what we did and saw on our trip to Yellowstone. I like journaling so much, I might even keep writing in this book after we get home.

Jasmine drew a picture of a moose to go with her entry. Then she put a speech bubble over its head and wrote, "Bye, Jasmine, come back soon!" When she showed her picture to Jesse, he laughed and said, "Maybe he will still be waiting for us next summer."

You Can Write a Journal, Too!

Journals aren't just for trips. You can start a journal anytime. There are many kinds of journals. A personal journal or diary is just for you. Or you can use a journal to write back and forth with a friend, teacher, or other adult. You can keep a journal to write down what you read and how you feel about it. Or you can write about what you learn in school and what you think about it. A journal can help you to think about the things that happen in your life. It is also a good way to make sure you remember events that are important to you.

As you start writing your journal, remember that a personal journal is something you do for yourself. You can write whatever you want because you don't have to show it to anyone. Use the following tips to help you start writing.

1. You don't need a fancy book to journal. Many people use spiral notebooks for their journals.

2. It is a good idea to find a quiet place to journal if you can.

3. Think about your day and what you want to write about before you begin. Remember, you don't have to write about everything that happened—just the things that are interesting or important to you.

4. You also don't have to write the same amount for every entry. Some days you might have a lot to write about, while on other days you might not.

5. You can also include photos, keepsakes like ticket stubs or party invitations, or pictures that you draw yourself.

6. If you run out of ideas for what to write about, try making a list or doing a Five-Minute Freewrite.

7. Don't forget to date each entry so you will remember when you wrote it.

Why not start a journal today?

Glossary

entry: the writing from one session of journaling.

personal journals: books of writing or drawings about a person's experiences and feelings, also called diaries.

private: something that is not shared with other people.

relates: how one thing connects to another.

For More Information

Books

Banks, Ann. *The Children's Travel Journal*. New York: The Little Bookroom, 2004.

Ganeri, Anita. *I Can Write Journals and Narratives*. Chicago: Heinemann, 2013.

Websites

Primary Journal Ideas
http://www.letteroftheweek.com/primary_journal_ideas.html
This website includes a huge list of fun journal prompts.

Journal Buddies
http://journalbuddies.com/
This website features ideas and tips for young journalists.

About the Author

In addition to writing in her journal, Rachel Lynette has written more than 100 books for children of all ages as well as resource materials for teachers. She also maintains *Minds in Bloom*, a blog for teachers and parents. When she isn't writing, she enjoys spending time with her family and friends, traveling, reading, drawing, crocheting colorful hats, biking, and playing racquetball.